CHAMELEON | NACHTROER

Charlotte Van den Broeck was born in Turnhout, Belgium, in 1991. After studies in English and German, she took a Masters in Drama at the Royal Conservatoire in Antwerp. She has published two collections of poetry in Dutch, *Kameleon* (2015), which was awarded the Herman de Coninck debut prize for poetry by a Flemish author, and *Nachtroer* (2017), which was nominated for the VSB Poetry Prize 2018 and the Ida Gerhard Prize. These two volumes are combined in *Chameleon | Nachtroer*, translated by David Colmer (Bloodaxe Books, 2020).

Her poetry has also been translated into German, Spanish, French, Serbian and Arabic. In 2016 she opened the Frankfurt Bookfair together with Dutch poet Arnon Grunberg. In 2017 she was one of that year's Versopolis poets, performing at several European festivals including Ledbury in Britain. As well as publishing critically acclaimed collections she is renowned for her distinctive performances, which differ from UK/US versions of spoken word as theatre pieces 'searching for the speakability and experience of oral poetry', now presented in English as well as Dutch.

Charlotte Van den Broeck

Chameleon | Nachtroer

Translated by
DAVID COLMER

BLOODAXE BOOKS

ISBN: 978 1 78037 447 5

First published 2020 by
Bloodaxe Books Ltd,
Eastburn,
South Park,
Hexham,
Northumberland NE46 1BS.

www.bloodaxebooks.com
For further information about Bloodaxe titles
please visit our website and join our mailing list
or write to the above address for a catalogue

Supported using public funding by
**ARTS COUNCIL
ENGLAND**

This book was published with the support of Flanders Literature
(www.flandersliterature.be).

**FLANDERS
LITERATURE**

Cover design: Neil Astley & Pamela Robertson-Pearce.

Printed in Great Britain by Bell & Bain Limited, Glasgow, Scotland, on
acid-free paper sourced from mills with FSC chain of custody certification.

CONTENTS

III Origin

NACHTROER

Eight, ∞

Nachtroer

'Slash and Burn' was published in January 2020 by *Asymptote*.

CHAMELEON

After nothing does the womanly desire to please strive so much as after the *appearance of the naive*; sufficient proof, even if we were to have no other, that the greatest power of the sex reposes in this property.

FRIEDRICH SCHILLER, *On Naïve and Sentimental Poetry*
tr. William F. Wertz, Jr.

I   The Red Cross on the Treasure Map

Bucharest

Some places are so small
they fit under a fingertip.
I try to point out where it was
but hardly know myself by now.

Still standing in the debris of forgetting
is my grandfather's bookcase and the Sunday afternoon
we read the atlas together, his finger
on the capital of Romania.

'A splendid collection of little whores they have there,' he said
and I thought a whore must be something like the Eiffel Tower
and was offended he'd never brought one home
for me in miniature.

Later borders and grandfathers turned out to be relative
only that afternoon is written in embossed letters
on the pages of the atlas as the afternoon
I still saw him as a first-rate guide.

Sisjön

Standing by the lake are a naked grandfather and a child.
We decide it's completely natural
staring politely at our toes as we step out of our clothes.

We force our cheeks up into smiles, the innocence
of my swimming costume disappears with a single glance.
Roguishly we glide into the water.

We swim to the other side, breaststroke
feeling strange without the lines of a swimming pool.
I talk about the way my mother's breasts float
in the bathwater and how that seems to contradict the laws of gravity.

On your sleeping bag we smoke cigarettes, my first.
My gums feel like a dried apricot pit
but I tell you I like it.

In the morning the sun burns us out early
we find the dead chick by the tent.
Whatever it was, it was defenceless.

Örebro

It is too cold to swim, we draw
bitter circles with our ankles, pushing
the water away from us, the lake's
midriff pushes back, rhythmic splashing
and pulling back and splashing once again.

The sound when we suck our feet out of the water
the sticking sand and the swaying stalks.
Your hands are tortoises, crawling ants.

Soon we will stop talking, no matter how minimal
our language, it destroys what we see.
What is left are holograms
conditional verbs.

I shudder, you cushion me with your arm, nothing too tender.
It is still breaking and it keeps breaking
into ever smaller pieces
the way bacteria divide.

It is too cold to swim, we draw
back into the tent, peel the skin
from each other's shoulders
gradually growing older.

Växjö

There is a lightness here that won't cooperate.
We're like two overtired children in the corner
of the playroom, pounding the rug with their fists
yelling that their bodies no longer fit their skin.

At noon we stare at the sun with bulging chameleon eyes.
The world blurs with clumsy swipes of crayon.
There is no perceptible difference between the hand and the table
only a transition of material.

In the dancing pixelated image
the girl's hair swings in long pigtails, girl's hair
that isn't yet a trump, but a pain when playing
when she walks, they're lashing whips.

Listlessness weighs down everything:
more mass on just as much surface
so that somewhere on the sides of the world
things fall off the edges.

There is a lightness here that won't cooperate.
As if it's all just a marble run
a course from up to down
till someone lifts us up again.

Japanese Pond

I am scared that my lower arms
will transform into my aunty's koi
covered with silver skin and
bright red birthmarks.

They will spasm
until they're hanging from my elbows
like limp members.

We walked past the chestnuts
where our legs gave up the ghost like inflatable boats
where our gulping fish mouths
kissed eczema rings on each other's skin.
We circled them with felt-tips.

We sent fingers out along the lines, searching
for overlapping patterns, resurfacing
furtively with pockets
full of exoskeletons.

Hvannadalshnúkur

Fingertips, suction pads, whatever else don't fall asleep now
if you don't fall asleep now, we can talk now
we can talk here, above these sheets
about the pale hills across the water
the clumps of grass in which we sat
in which we did not yet sit together, summers
we experienced separately, the lightening of our hair
the lengthening of the days, here, above these sheets

whatever else don't break now, the scorpions in my bookcase
are abroad tonight, it is safe now, the warmth
on the windows, the mist on your stories, it is almost
morning above these sheets a final hour, here
in my languid loins, stay, keep on talking now
in my body's languid loins

about: abdominal cavities, the silly season, the distant country in my ears
the boughs of sturdy trees past the sounds of words
here, fever dreams, here, above these sheets gnarled hands
and bowls of thirst, white lilies for the living-room, the walls
forgotten blueprints, the innocence of earthworms
in a child's mouth, we can talk here, above these sheets.

August

Steel arms close around us
from now on nothing separate, no one
needs to be afraid of dying alone
and clamped into a recliner.

We assign our body parts new functions
swallowing the strangled gasps in our throats
until they start to pound again inside us, deep
stereo from belly-button to belly-button.

On the bridge the little sirens take turns
to lift their T-shirts for the truck drivers
here they smear butter on burns
and maize pops from the barrels of air guns.

Choose a focal point, the magnifying glass
is aimed at us, nothing is small enough
to lose in the funfair the manic boys
can't get enough, more and more like Sisyphus.

Dear mothers, don't worry, all hunger shrinks
in the end we'll lick coagulated gravy out of the buffet trays, promise
and when the dog's on heat
we'll take her back to the shelter, promise.

I ask myself: does the cellophane of our skin melt
from the heat of the sun or is the warmth we feel
a rotting from the inside out?

Was it like that with our copper birdcage too
two rusty canaries on the floor?
A newspaper headline about increasing mastectomies
leaking from their beaks.

They said the children would fluff up the pillows.
They haven't had stuffed Pikachus at the sideshows for years.
We covered our parents with wood shavings.

Sampling

A woman holds a dog on her lap
by the scruff of its neck as if it's a handbag.

A woman takes a packet of dried sausage
out of her handbag.

A woman plays with her handbag during a job interview
and may be having a sexual fantasy.

A woman zips herself into the inside pocket
of another woman's handbag.

A woman loses her handbag
and accuses a Moroccan.

A woman collects cigarette butts and has by now
accumulated the volume of a small handbag.

A woman has collected so many handbags
that a magazine does a feature on her and her handbags.

Diagnosis

I am cut with someone who likes to look into the light
and a sad soloist in search of the simplicity
of a man at the bread dispenser on a Sunday evening.

Behind my street with its council flats
there is an avenue with plane trees and family cars
so quiet, as if no one here ever pulls hard on a leash
to choke a dog.

The third house on the right is home to an Indian
with a Volvo. Nobody talks to him
but people suspect he's a good cook
because he kills his own chickens.

The man at the bread dispenser has corduroy eyebrows.
I won't have enough courage to lay my hand very briefly
on his forehead, I am too young
to have things of my own.

Fish Bowl

I have a tendency to make a round shape
with my hands
when talking about totality

to want to slide the emptiness between my hands over
the bald spot of the man in front of me in the tram.

As if there's anything at all there
I would consider complete.

Gilles

Of all things I keep pineapple in medium syrup
in my canned-goods head, a museum
with overpriced admission, only
Watteau's *Gilles* hanging on the walls.

Of all things I keep children's parties
and a ketchup mouth, my first love
in formaldehyde (he bought me a skipping rope)
and later, razor-sharp, scalpels, lancets
the swearwords, the credit-consuming-cheating.

Us, no more than a tint in some dark blue
and me, wishing I knew how to candy.
Us with added sugar –
that must be delicious.

Flamingo

I sleep the way flamingos stand:
with one leg straight, the other
bent at the knee against my lower belly
like a folded white stick.

On this down bed, unsteady in dark pink
still stretched out neck to neck
we gradually turned into two entangled
sausages, gasping for breath.

Flamingos conquer each other synchronously
a genteel courtship display, lasting at least
twelve lashed glances a whole monogamous life.

A joust we mainly know from TV shows.

First we were still grey
now we are almost pilots
almost an ode to birds.

The North Sea

Faraway on the breakwater you find
an unsteady balance with your arms
at the end of distance you shout

trembling soundwaves in concentric circles.
The outermost rings prove what is beautiful
and good and true: hyperbole
at odds with reality.

The house looks like a hotel room
where we recover from ourselves on a brief
stopover between birthmarks
and mediocrity.

Charlotte Cake

When you turned over and we tried in vain
to make a dessert from our jelly legs
I knew you couldn't bear me anymore.

Though I come in all kinds of flavours:
    – Charlotte with raspberry mousse.
    – Charlotte with orange and mint cream.
    – Cherry Charlotte.
    – Eggnog Charlotte.
    – Burgundian ham Charlotte
No?

The idiotically romantic way I tried to count
the freckles on your left shoulder-blade,
too many to keep track of, when

we didn't even say goodbye, after which you never
said 'hello' again either, you blurting out
that I was junk food, raised
and slaughtered on a McDonald's farm where they turn
beautiful calves into cheap hamburgers.

I am your big-and-tasty-quarter-pounder-BBQ-bacon-
southern-style-crispy-chicken-
premium-grilled-double-cheeseburger.

Am I tasty, do you want some more?

When I smile,
the outline of my face changes,
look.

I don't know what you find the most beautiful,
but happiness is within reach
according to certain sections of bookshops
so mould my face
into whichever shape
is most like the mask in your comedy.

I am less tragic than you think.

II Discovery Channel

People Who Watch Wildlife Films to Better Understand Themselves

We watch wildlife films:
sexually mature female on the savannah
on the sofa we plan an educational trip
from one body to another.

Arms pulled out of the dress, setting
each other in motion, finding
a rhythm, lying motionless
under your hands.

Speaking is just camouflage for forgetting
let's never turn this into language
let's steal the numbers from these clocks
and the clocks from the walls
until they're only circles,
unable to rob us of anything.

Only this remote moment
in which we lost our shape.
According to the laws of reciprocity
it can always come back to the beginning

arms out of the dress again, setting
each other in motion
finding a rhythm.

Grand Jeté

A kick in the back of the knee, that's what it feels like
sometimes when I'm bending over you and I don't have

to hold back bones in this soft body. My spine doesn't snap,
a stubborn bamboo that makes me bend so far

I can keep on bending until you kiss another bend into
my limbs. Side to side we swerve in and out of each other,

we swerve over each other's borderlines until I just can't tell
where body ends and landscape begins. A plain as far

as the eye can see and past all sight us sloping further
into each other on the edge of this pliant house of skin.

A moment stretching out in a music box seen through a peephole.
If we wind it up it plays again:

a girl dancing with one arm raised and the other making
a bowl in which you turn to liquid. You think it passes

but we will keep it up for years until we bend so far,
so far and the bamboo snaps.

Whalespotting

Sleep creeps under the skin of our deflated bodies
filling us to the brim
sandbags against drowning.

We sink anyway
drinking the air with our muscles
like only whales can, mastodons

wandering through the dark room we stare up
at a ceiling of water, a lucid languid mirror
for our waking consciousness.

The creases in the sheets
draw maps on this ossified body
over and over again

we must force movement back into it
prying ourselves out of the pale tentacles
of a nameless monster.

Satellite Photo

Whale bones have been found
in the east of Russia.

The carcass on the beach
plays God
the ribs taller
than the tallest man in town.

I too want something holy and infinite
a skeleton on which to braid my sorrow.

For days I sat on a beach
hands cupped over my ears like shells.

In long, low notes
that's how whales cry.

Small Volcano

We dropped an anchor, saying, All Reason ends here.
If we ever wanted to think again
we could return to that anchor.

'Now' is a click of the fingers, 'now' is already gone.
So if we now forget that we are passing this place
we are an eternity, we are the sheets over the head
lords and masters of time.

As long as we don't breathe
we won't pass and won't need to think of
why should we ever again think of

raspberries and red wine, illicit love-making
a hand that doesn't know where, a hand that accidentally
gets a memory, a click of the fingers, a pastime
the clack of a pinched tongue

or the red uvula that whips what's caught in a throat
down, ever further, your eyes
black beads
ever further down
little black beads
I pick them out of my belly-button
buccaneer pearls.

Seraphic Light

A pelican beak opens wide over the top
and bottom of my entire body, that's how small I am
a man, who pulls off his cowboy boots
and turns into a fish, writhing left and right
on the bed slapping the duvet as if
begging mercy in a wrestling match.

Every slap of the fishbody sends flakes of skin
flying, at every slap a gymnast, hands thick with chalk
pushes off in my head, the limber memory of all
I have discarded thuds; the gliding motorways
the clothes and oaths, every broken promise
every toppled sugar bowl.

All the times I didn't stand straight I was wasting inches.
I have never learned how to take a position only
to open wide and let out a harsh
sound, that's how small I am.

The retina projects a fruit fly
on the side of my right eye
adding a full stop at the end of every image
I perceive. As if left to right
and stop motion is the only way I can see:

A man with a double chin stop
The man inflates his chin stop
The chin expands until it's a pouch stop
The man waddles down the street with his gigantic pouch stop
The man falls over into a puddle from the weight of his pouch stop
The man does not have webbed feet stop

I close my eyes, leaving him to thrash around
and still see the fruit fly; dark with a little dark spot in it
that's how small I am.

I pull curtains across curtains across eyelids
in the assumption that the spot too
will dissolve in so little light.
It's still there.

Tyrant

We try to telekinetically outstare each other
at the statue of Goethe.

No movement.

Our gazes are empty oyster shells
the tongue that slurped them out forgotten
along with how salty the skin, how the screeching
sounded again and, was it somehow
like the silence of an abyss
or was it softer?

In the hotel room we drop
the way a horse stops trotting
front legs first
then smacking the rug with its teeth.

We yell the alphabet into the crevasse
between our mouths, every echo
ending at a Scrabble tile
that's how we make words, at a pinch
thirst, avalanche, tusk.

Chameleon [I]

The room's running a temperature and night is the patchwork quilt.
First the call and then the quivering, and so we wait
backs aimed at each other like two
high-strung bows.

I could do it, I could pop your backbone
like bubble wrap.

We will probably lose all substance anyway
that which is permanent in the things that change
but everything changes and nothing
remains equal to itself, we too
change, slowing down
growing scales on our shoulder-blades.

We curl up our tongues until our mouths are full
of loosed silence. In the terrarium the female chameleon starts to glow.
She takes on the colour of post-coital cheeks
of men whose only postcard home goes to their local pub.

The kind of red that only comes in shades of shame.

Chameleon [II]

I speak in melodious tones of 'here' and 'now' and 'stay'
and repeat it so often it starts to grate
until you roll me back into your mouth midsentence
laying me on your tongue, which undulates softly
the way little girls who are overweight undulate
softly while walking.

And I want you to say me again, that you can't stop saying me
so that I break out of the hollow of your mouth
and you give me new names, the wrong ones
like 'sweet' and 'small' and 'slow'
and I begin to act accordingly like a conditioned dog,
covering my breasts
when you come into the bathroom unexpectedly.

Let us lie our analogue love into this pillow
somewhere between tongue and teeth.
Maybe we will occur to each other after all.
Maybe we will remember where exactly
the shuddering began
when we lost the rhythm.

Felidae [I]

We drive to the edge with carcasses in the back of the car.
Claws retracted, you treat me to a bit of excess, sometimes
you say it's consolation, sometimes that it's creaking.

The darkness of the motorway is never as lonely
as the tunnel's orange light.
To look at each other is to rob each other
to tear each other's throat.

Your fingers press deeper into the wet plaster
of my shoulder-blades.
Let this back be the unwritten landscape
you later call your motherland.
Let's invent our myths of origin right here and now.
Even stray toms need a name.

You said hands had never held your head like this before
never before had a woman turned
into a cat before your eyes.

Felidae [II]

We don't know where from
or how it overwhelms us
only that it stretches out
in the seconds between the falling beams
of the motorway lights and tangles into me.

Your shoulder-blades stick out so sharply
the bones form a skull
that looks at me with reproach
for knowing so little beyond what I perceive
and what I perceive is at the mercy
of the chameleon in my head that licks
everything to camouflage.

A bluish-black cat crosses the motorway
up to the pine trees, back home
we don't turn on the lights, we lose ourselves
in the stalking of our thoughts
mouths hurtling under car tyres.

Rorschach

A line runs through me, an ugly hang
for instability, at least it does that morning
with the bulging sabre-toothed tit
when I want something

with a rewind button if possible
to stretch into a memory
a greater sorrow than the meaningless
swell of old sound in shells.

When I bump myself I want to know what shape
the bruise will take
whether there's still some symbolism to be wrung
from threadbare longing, I don't know, except

that your whole face gathers
in your lips, even now
opening, pink lotus mouth
your candy-floss temple

the cantilever action with which
I throw my head back for you –
better for raptures. Imagine:

no longer needing to balance there
where latitude and longitude cross.
If something doesn't know its place
can it take place

and where?

Astrology for Beginners

Kilometres under the crust
the burning Earth proves its roundness.

In the same way we too will one day
coincide: hardly woman almost man
in a unisex mac.

The look in your eyes, thinking my skirt down to my ankles.
My skin that now recognises no fingers but yours.

The day we ran over a hare and tried to read
the origins of grief in its guts.
We were scared it would never dry.

Maybe there's an answer in the eye of the telescope.
An explanatory regularity in the orbit of Venus.

Night after night we watched.
We only saw halogen lights in an empty sky.

Space Peel

Under the blanket of orange fleece, we
according to immutable laws of our own
are ants on a mandarin peel

only taking what we require, nothing
needs to happen in a reality
that isn't going anywhere.

Making the sign disappear in the significance.
The scab marks and hides the wound.
We will speak a double, greedy tongue.

Instructions

Forgetting
is circular reasoning.

Put a spanner in the works,
do it.

Don't bump anything
over the edge of this head.

Lampyridae

Did you think it would be this small:
the travel version of a longing
no larger than the palm of a hand

glow-worm buckling at the knees
under the weight of its Latin name
triple word score.

Looking into the light with our eyes screwed up, the blank
spaces in the encyclopaedia contain all the knowledge
we need, something that somehow

dazzles, something that says
you don't need to know what it is
to pick it up.

Expedition

With soft puffs of breath you scratch
my cheeks bloody, you fold
my hands into origami elephants
paper feet marching

to a guilty landscape, the memory
woven so tightly into the skin
we search in vain for where
it's torn us open.

We think of home, briefly,
staccato.
Just long enough
to feel the distance
we've let ourselves get carried away.

Archaeological Site

I carve you from marble, quickly nipping you on the shoulder
my teeth scraping over your marble shoulder.

No matter how often I hack you out of the chalk cliffs of my mind
you hardly seem to fit into any memories.

Sometimes through the cracks in the day I still find your boyish eyes
the saffron we sprinkled on our lips, more often

you walk beyond the reach of my imagination
past the atlas moth and then I hack and hack

you out of those chalk cliffs again and screech that since the start of humankind we
that's what you said, that since the start of humankind we

have been licking the honey out of each other's hair, the light refracts on the bathtub
mixing with the foam on this rash motionless water

in which I score the final lines, laying your hands in a triangle
offset against the gentle curve of your hips.

I pin an atlas moth to your chest.

Hunter/Gatherer

With your last savings you went online
and bought a collection of fossils.

They turned out to be made in China. Since then
you've been lying on the bed like a starfish, arms and legs wide

turning to stone. I cut myself on you
walking past to hush the mollusc

in your head. I say, 'There will be something left.
Even molecules leave fingerprints in space.'

I'm not so sure. I search and search our bedroom
sown with pairs of odd socks and numbers

to three decimal places, nothing else that proves
the proposition, no curl of the lip

no black lace négligée or shepherd dog
to muster everything we've lost

taking it in its jaws, shaking it back and forth
until it's not afraid, until it's stopped thrashing.

Think of light in a dark room and your pupils
will contract all the same, petrified boy

with your limbs spread-eagled, flared
nostrils so close to the track, think

of the branches we used to poke the anthill
until enough was destroyed, think of the centre of the universe and stop

shaking, the universe doesn't have a centre
only a viewpoint, think of the woman

you saw before you when masturbating for the first time, think
of how she exploded in the quivering light of the desk lamp, think

of the folded ideals under your slogan-blazoned T-shirts
of the cutting predictability of a clock, of all

that is round and empty: a fist that doesn't know why it is being raised
photos of fat girls with pink guns in America.

There will be something left.

Triceratops

We look at the flat white stones on the beach,
finding no beauty in the object
or the idea behind it.

Once in Arizona you stood with your toes curled
around the edge of a crater: never before had you looked so deep
into the place you wanted to put my face.

Skin that isn't touched changes into a scab
the sliding tectonic plates of your nervous system
make you spin inside

until you are dizzy
and reaching out
to a blur of light and colour.

On the way back
you bought a plastic dinosaur at the gas station.
That's when I knew we wouldn't keep the car on the road.

The crash won't hurl us back.

III   Origin

Specialist Poulterer

Women make broth of themselves in the bath
until their insides simmer out in the form of a child.

This is how we are born: without a shell,
without a reassurance that one day we will find

a mouth so like our own
that we will speak through it.

We too will end up splay-legged
in the tub with clucking breath

and the nervous tic of a wobbling head
on a groggy body

while the water runs away in circles,
a tiny swirling tornado
that won't even make the weather report.

Bull's Head

Since my birth, an enormous bull's head has raged
in my mother's belly. It storms through her abandoned body

gouging scars in the fallow mother, sometimes
she doesn't quite know who I am, this is disconcerting

as she was once a perfect fit, fortunately I am
according to the astronomical constellation Cancer

reliable, creative and hedonistic. She clings to that,
proof of a god between heaven and her waters.

When we had baked chicory and ham, I got the cheese crust.
All of it. Because I wanted it.

For me love comes out of a saucepan
always two dollops more on a full plate

a second biscuit hidden in the custard.
That is a common form of maternal behaviour:

'Stuffing the kid.'
Feeling the hollow I'd left in her, she wanted me full and round.

One morning I announced my budding breasts.
She was a mess for days on end.

Finally I got a bra
one with *Hello Kitty* on it.

Inside her belly the snorting bull's head thumped.
A hollow only becomes a hole when nothing else fits it.

Slowly we fossilised into two separate creatures.
It's hard to say

which of us became the insect
and which the amber.

Netezon Laundrette

My mother cries while doing the washing.

This is the perfect moment for mothers to cry
because a revolving washing-machine drum
generally makes a racket.
I do hear her sobs, but they are so soft
they could be background noise.

A washing machine licks the day's wounds.
You can stuff in everything that doesn't fit in your head.
Sheets that haven't been slept on, for instance.
Or the tobacco smell in your cancer-patient grandfather's coat.
Long programme, sixty degrees, cleansing ritual.

For a long time I thought it wasn't fair that I had a mother who cried.
As if I had to go to school with a heavier bag
and singing Ring a Ring o' Roses I always thought
the tissue must be for my mother.

I explained the phenomenon of 'the crying mother' from the suspicion
that there wasn't enough water and that was why she stared into the machine
and thought long and hard about dead kittens, until
she could do the washing with her tears.

I grew up with salt rings in my clothes.

Ausflug/Auszug

We take a room in a local womb.
Here for a moment my mother and I can be each other's everything.
What's more we're writing history:
never before has anyone gone back so close to the source.

We know we can't stay long
all possible forms of holiday come to an end.
That's why we arrange our things as in a hospital room,
restrained and temporary.

When the big body around us sleeps
and the heartbeat slows, we tell each other the story
of Jonah in the belly of the whale. For three days
and three nights, in the belly of the whale. We find it hilarious
cracking up like girls.

On the postcard we write that it is a small
yet pleasant place to stay,
that the days are like circles and the weather surprisingly good,
and that we in the meantime have grown so similar
you can hardly tell the girl from the mother.

Winter Veg

Her hands are chicory, pulled
fresh from the ground.

The green imprint of the scant light
still showing around her wrists.

Sometimes she retires to a dark room
long before grown-up bedtime.

I spoon up the soup and she stares,
I spoon, she stares
a diagonal of silence
across the kitchen table.

I learn a second language
in which sighs are nouns.

We know that plants breathe.
Nobody else here ever sucks
the oxygen out of the rooms.

Since then we've kept cactuses
on the sills and ledges.

Council Flat

My grandmother sneaks into the scullery
to try on the wedding-ring from her first marriage.

If you leave something unsaid,
it hasn't necessarily happened.

Over the years she has learnt to reconcile herself
to the semantics of silence, holding her tongue

to the rhythmic tick of her sewing-machine,
taking in, letting out, taking up, *letting go*

now and then into the scullery to see
if she can still squeeze her finger into the past.

Our is just a possessive pronoun,
a house built of language with no end of other names.

It is hard to live in three letters.
There is so little room.

Turtle Reflex

She has turned in on herself, head pulled back
hands folded and the folded hands on her lap
stalled on their way to feel the fabric of her skirt
as if it's out of reach.

I am moulded into starched and ironed frocks
like something you keep fresh in silver paper.
A child of two, still bald, a hairband
with a bow to clarify my sex.
Despite these measures they still
call me 'a sweet little boy'.

Round and round she turns with her stiff joints
grandma in a see-through top in front of the street organ
the boy next door turns a tortoise upside down
she whirls and whirls.

There are only a limited number of words
to describe a texture, maybe
that is why she is so slow
to touch the fabric of her skirt, maybe
she wants to run through everything that was ever 'soft' first
to make sure this is the right word.

Genealogy

A tongue licks a finger, the wind
only touches one side

the finger stirs the resin in the womb
stripping the membranes

and I force myself on the world.
Later in changing-rooms I point

accusations at kids with outies
because they're still carrying a bit of mum

and mum's a stone. They will sink
in the pool, but I don't say so.

That is how we thread ourselves together
with the amber remnants from a previous body.

I am no follower.

Fernweh

On the island a woman reaches out
for the suspicion of an elsewhere.

Sometimes the suspicion takes the form of a bird
leaving a trail in the air.

She takes the trail between thumb and finger
securing the end to a woman in the port

who holds it in her fingertips the exact same way,
a filament that, somewhere inside of her,

sets off a longing for a remote place
where people leave the rest of the world unspoken

where people grip children around the hips
or launch them in canoes.

NACHTROER

Where will the sun be when the sky is black?
You will have all night to ponder about that

DANIEL NORGREN, 'Why may I not go out and climb the trees'

The inner life, the I, separation are uprootedness itself, non-participation, and consequently the ambivalent possibility of error and of truth. The knowing subject is not a part of a whole, for it is limitrophe of nothing.

EMMANUEL LEVINAS, *Totality and Infinity*
tr. Alphonso Lingis

Eight, ∞

VIII

don't lean too far now the evening is squeezing out the light and our breath
bump-blue the skin, the pounded war drum for the shortfall inside of us
the house submits to being divided into banana boxes and possessive pronouns
the bookcase into left and right
yours the maps, the Russians and the complete Márquez
I get dictionaries in all languages, biographies of dictators
and yes, poetry, now of all times refusing to speak, you ask:
which bird was it that tears its own breast with its beak?
the pelican gets no further than the tip of my tongue
now I know that mourning starts by bumping your elbow
and radiates into your fingers
pre-emptive anaesthesia before they touch again

VII

something in the body will pulse for hours after the shot
until that too runs out, the memory of a heartbeat
which animal did we say we wanted to hit?
We were always hunting each other in ourselves
is that what we really became? salted and hung
our ration of ideals, an aerial photo of the site as it was
where we were going to finally forgive ourselves to each other, when?
even writing is dying out, my hand drags
left, pulling me backwards into years that are gone
into your armpit a foxhole with time to reflect, where I found the hollow
big enough for all my shortcomings, that's when I did it
deliberately turning you and me into parts from a scale model kit

VI

a magician saws me in two and opens me up
to the audience, my empty trunk revealed after the night, after the battle
in which I became a general and a mortal, lost ground and organs
forgot you because of the trumpets from the parade inside of me
looking back I could already see how you'd take your coat off the rack
a small parting gesture, disappointment between your shoulder-blades
and still I marched further into the depths, past the submerged rock
where I dissolved in regret – of course, what else would I dissolve into
if not a groaning sound? it betrays me on stage
everyone looks, I blurt out 'darling' and 'wrong' and
'forgive me', but the applause goes on forever
afterwards no one sews me up

V

Europe, an interchangeable landscape outside the car windows, subordinate
to whatever's playing on the radio, to what's running through our minds as we stare
at the motorway, a cadence of churches, Czechs and distance that repeats itself
the way that we for years now, unwittingly but doggedly, have been repeating ourselves
Vienna becomes our living-room, the Danube a pinched nerve, even love-making
tedious in the dry heat, I swallow mosquitoes, always and later
two points in time that choke me up, now that they are undeniable and here
more than ever we are the cast of our happiness and not the happiness itself
which slides by past the signs with the names of towns, past the tingling
and the doubt, and then at the rest area, the gentle stasis of each other's smile
concealing a scream that pleads for us to never forget
the secret alliance, what stirs us and the noose

IV

outside the storm bends the palm trees low, for seven days a cottage
on Lanzarote forms a cocoon against the cold at home in February
in the daytime we catch up on sleep for nights in which our seething bodies
– reckless and twenty – imitate the island's volcanoes
we have resolved ourselves to a life in Mondrian colours
flame-red the love, the water stretched out, the excess of yellow flowers
on the kitchen table, that's all, a negative of what will really happen:
everything is building, decline and boredom, but we evade
the ways of stopping, if necessary we will choose stasis ourselves
but no one's going to smash our windows from outside and yes
the rain's a cage but not as real as the cage we read about in books
where people – beyond us in all things – can't help but lose to each other

III

by now your name the prelude to all things, getting up, speaking
and moving, I am a marionette moved by your breath, you are gone
and the day changes into something that must be borne, absence
a word with a leash, I wait for thicker skin and mastery
what kind of biology prescribes symbiosis for one alone?
it is unbearable, the cold half, the eagle's eye that dives into me
in search of an opposite, until you're home and once again persist in everything
a sniper in a defenceless kingdom where we tolerate the dragging
weekdays without armour or cramps
the open kitchen window shows a robin lying
motionless in the passage, you take me on your lap
death hasn't entered our thoughts

II

writing all those letters, bedside cabinets full, what did it prove
a craving for significance, a prayer in clammy phrases
leaves us as we were: sixteen and seventeen and lost to each other
leave us our blinkers and in our letters the reality
resembling in so many ways the warmth of sleep
so we can reach the dream, grown older in the meantime
and woken up and prevented and who has been banished who banishes
now distance is no longer separation but the separation
has taken on the constraint of something that will no longer turn
in retrospect it's cruel to want to measure loneliness
and each other against the Milky Way, to the moon and back I said
still meaning every mile, and yet

I

Lying in the field are a boy and a girl who stir memories of before
I suspect they're us, eight years ago, but they look so much like strangers
that I don't walk up to warn them they've remembered it all wrong
there were no birds flying overhead that day, no snow or ice on the field, October still
the reeds around the nearby pond were dry and hacked, in the background
at intervals the sound of a car on the road, otherwise nothing
I don't tell them that here between the last mosquitoes and the first kisses
they will come up with names for the kids, that the shipyard has become
a silicone factory in the meantime, or that he should let go of her hand now
to get used to later, when they will only touch each other by accident and awkwardly
I don't say anything, because it was exactly like that, the way they're lying there:
the surrender, the blind light of afternoon and later the poems about it

Nachtroer

Nachtroer

(for Remco Campert)

Evening
and the glow-stick's in your eyes and you are looking
its orange snapped into your eyes the liquid light
in which I knew what I would never know again
the way a word

can come to mean another word
just like that and how it all

outside the evening's heavy in the air, stale and already late
the sluggish smoke irresolute between us, and you
looking and what that stirs in an evening, in me, bright red ants
hundreds for a second before the light shrinks, the itch
the raging itch in your eyes that will not ease

not even now the light

because on the slipway between now and later
a room awaits with neither doubt nor mosquitoes
how else could it be with your hand dangling over me

not touching but giving me the possibility
of pushing up against it the boundless possibility
of pushing up against a hand that is not touching
me, but giving me the possibility to

waiting and swelling
are almost the same, bleeding into each other
at the tipping point of what I want
what I know in the fluorescent light

the spectrum in a puddle for a moment
it was true and bright orange
sometimes it can't be any other way

in my mind I expand the hand with an evening
a mouth a shoulder a crotch
and that it all

and you don't let the ants and the swelling colours
that colour is only dust and light that the light can hardly
the evening still bright orange

leave it a while

until the light no longer until the looking too
is only the direction of your eyes

Haematoma

The way it goes
when two of the Earth's plates collide
does an island really rise up out of the ocean

or does the pressure breach a bed
that is not even the bottom
but the surface for a deeper gash, no skin left

eczema covered with tattoos, the garden filled with cypresses
and gradually getting too cold for mosquitoes – for you
a relief no doubt, here the itch still burns

their squashed bodies scarring the walls, proof
that you were here and that once I must have known
the difference between a shock and a caress

Drift

One more hour and one more and one more
and still no morning

some kind of gentle rain on the window
beyond it the first traffic, the rustling around me swelling
into a new space, an instant ocean
sounding like the sea on relaxation CDs: surrounding you
completely
until light empties the room

and it almost seems like surviving:
wanting to give everything a territory and a time
people, intelligible physics

shear for instance
the way wind scouring the surface of the water
moves particles and later it doesn't even matter
the volume unchanged, not patterning the blue

does it matter
who grabbed what where
or who was the last left standing?

facts are always overtaken by structures, the teeth
ground to grit of a morning, the mouth emptied of pleas

and last night I did try
to throw the fish on the beach back into the water I tried
to throw them back and into life and again to throw
the fish back into life in the water I tried

does it matter, stretching arms together
into emptiness? there is almost

no air between the past and bones and sheets
all we're made of in the end

continental breakfast in bed, illusion of a place
that could be ours without a chimney or a guard dog or eyes

but we don't live anywhere
unless it's hotel rooms or the crematorium

and it's the people who pass and the animals who die
each its own kind of coup de grâce, equally helpless
the last, crooked twist

of the mouth, the day stretching out
into a long, long night, awake
with thoughts of before, an old compulsive rage

the wandering lasts
longer than the horoscope promised

longer than it takes for streets to find new routes
to redesign a city, uncoupled
from memory, from the phony yellow of streetlights
that even make a goodbye glow

and it's not what I want, instead
I choose an organ you can pawn
turning in the sheets so often you turn too
and a triangle becomes a line

eagle and prey not a law, just a game

when the morning comes, traffic taking off
and that razor light

pick up the teeth
leave the fish

Aquarium

Look
above the wheezing city our faces tremble in the hotel window
quivering blue and printed with previous mouths

not having travelled far enough
to reckon what's past a phenomenon
it lies between us, crying for form and breath

and I mustn't fall asleep
I have to free you, night after night
I swim a line from left to right
not even a constellation

Blue

A voice is out hunting tonight

now a date falls on a date and just like this day a year ago driving rain
just like a year ago today on the E17 eastbound all lanes closed
in both directions because of a crash, today too thinking
too much about circles, suspicious

of what moves in that meek form
like birds of prey and cyclones, clocks and progeny

almost as if
the year that took so long to be over hasn't even passed
confusing difficulty with stasis after all

the shot gasps tonight
pursuing the voice, climbing the throat a creeper choking
what is so hard to say, all this time

searching for a better word for blue
because the sea is not enough and neither is the sky
nor your eyes nor October nor the seventh chords

even the infinite
even what surpasses imagining the infinite is not enough
nor the ink nor even consolation

searching for a better word for blue, day in day out
building model boats in case of a deluge that won't even wash
us out of our failings

what to do now the circle is starting again to round off as expected
replace atoms with monads after all
appease the scream with metaphors?

shall we finally give up
wanting to stare the stars off course at night, before we ever
reach the light they'll have long forgotten us
which way then?

a voice is out hunting tonight, lie still
and don't hear a thing

happiness is noiseless
don't hear a thing and hear how it creeps through us
in its socks, so quiet is its creeping through us
didn't even hear how it could grow so quiet
so taciturn

it's covered the throat with bark
and the voice rasps its way up

rubbed raw it breaks
out of the throat in accusations

what to say now the circle is leaving again
and meanwhile sad things have a birthday on the calendar

just like a year ago today lie down breech and turn to stone
and undo nothing, today too everything will continue
to stubbornly move from now to now to now

today too looking for the blue in the sea and in the blue
the image of us that gradually becomes dark and ink and reflection

the moon and her pale LED light
never yet has she let slip the truth to me

I held my head underwater, under the reflection
screaming for breath again in the empty sky
for nothing

succumb to rotation after all now the circle is back?
break the dead branches and shave old kisses from cheeks
time now to lay aside what is only paper, soon
tilting into the start of a new year

licking pollen from fingers come spring
taking a detour and making a plural, swinging
from body around loins around and around

in sloshed circles, the swoop, the whirlpool, the nadir
lying still

Lethe

A stroke away from if and later, a touch does not
evoke expectation of connection, that fallacy belongs
to another generation, always the same metaphor:

all those boxes with all those kinds of cereal in the supermarket
mild desperation packed in a hierarchy of preference
taming repetition

all movement begins with resistance, push back
until you realise that everything you wanted and did not want
and everything you will want is just an impulse

what is cherished is locked away behind passwords
and out of reach of the polyps of this or that desire
jittering up or down, storm or roars of laughter

as required, distance means haste
for a lover on speed dial in another city
in the space between two tones

the stubborn trembling hope that something will open in the silence
a siren singing glue, finally a lullaby
a meaningless paradox that points the way

to a boat ride and a ramshackle moon
from here the drowsy compass indicates a bed
a possible course

to drink from a river and forget
and all at once it seems so simple, subdued
the thirst for nothingness, raise the glass

Groceries Soft Drinks Spirits & Tobacco

between the rope lights, the comfort of a gleaming buying power
a Pakistani in stock all night long
ferryman at the gate to one more hour

and when that hour's gone the quay leaves the city behind
your body dissolves like an Alka-Seltzer
in the bruised beats pounding on your hips
at last you are almost

but a stranger calls out *drenkeling*
giving you your most fatal name
because the word makes no distinction
between falling overboard and having drowned

later still in the ice hole of your face
you see a howl behind your eyes
seismographed restlessness trembling through your body
from dark till dawn

passing in a dismal striptease
and again the light that makes you pale, the shipwreck
of the loins – as if there's nowhere else
for us to break

the rush, the sea, the other planets
it's never the middle but what surrounds it

like skin around the wreckage of your skeleton
splintered into bits of K'Nex, in a colourless afternoon
your head feels like a cat box and you wait

until your limbs click like clockwork
so effortlessly
do legs remember locomotion

so quickly do resolutions melt
under the incubator lamps of the streetlights
in late heat wandering again through what is impossible
and therefore urgent

from front door to late-night shop to front door
to the mouth of the volcano, postponing
sleep beside him

cigarettes and paprika crisps, a can of discount beer
that's always the last but one, you
were almost finally

but you don't complete yourself

because someone who wants to be an explorer doesn't wedge herself
between the degrees of latitude of two arms
where she can teem or hug
but will never run up a flag

someone who wants to be an explorer
knows how to use the skin as a pop up tent

eats dishes from distant regions
without thinking of her own grandmother's
kitchen, only ever dreamt of a camper
and not a destination, has lived her whole life
as a stable hand in a furnished garage

and yes, on the road you lose
a little mother tongue, a little shoe-leather, you leave
your lover behind in panoramic photos, eternally waving to happiness,
the sun and the loanwords from a mountaintop in Italy

but that was all before you knew
that it's not the teeth, but a yawn
that will devour the world

The Age of Aquarius

I was electricity last night, moving
and blue and everywhere and speed furious
through synapses and nerves lightning
in the power point in high-tension wires fire
and charge and heat tonight height and techno
circulation rewound sexless tonight
and the pupil's scope shattered crackling
possessed and climax and higher still the place
where the voice breaks in overtones a constellation
tonight moved and aimless unallowed further
than the milometer, further than an immeasurable distance
seen from above how cars roll over in submission
how motorways wear off the maps those who could
drove to a summer house the rest disappeared
swallowed first by sirens later in the mouths
of demagogues – their tongues forked into pro and anti
literature has taught us this:
there are people who [...] and there are people who [...]

I am a person who

I hit something, I think, I don't know what
or why I didn't swerve, don't know if
it matters, what if it touched me first
when I shrunk to two hands on a wheel
a reaction too late, a shock
lifted me up, awake again human again
and locked up in the wiring of my ribcage
on how many legs did it drag itself to the shoulder
did it look into the headlights first, if so how long
seconds extended with desperation
or was it always looking, is it still now
now the night is long and like a fluorescent tube
ticking, ticking and sparking, until it finally flicks on
in the morning and finally the white-out light
erases the fierce eyes from the headlights?

Leave the roaring animals
carry me to the hunters, when the time comes
do not watch as I put my hair up
and the bare throat betrays an open place
where no one hears a voice smashing
against what we exclude from language
better I had remained silent
then with time the stones would have
learnt to flower, one day the centrifuge
will separate the dust from the milk
I hope so, but either way the canary's song
machine-guns the light that shone
so simply through the white goblets
in the flint glass in the morning
I drink the dull milk and do not know
why I can't stop thinking of shards
I mustn't have enough

We are born separate
grow in our sleep up the stick in our back
entwining the backbone like creepers into the head sometimes
we branch off into another, in a milder winter
I hope so at least with my back tied to a stick
I hope for parataxis and that it's not too late
for similes, that something is still always like
something else like before like birds or simply
like flowers and oh, those few sounds
you can never shake: the test alarm
at the nuclear power station, the voice of a father
shut down by cancer reduced to a lump in his throat
and then that one time on the way to Ostend
as if a tree trunk passed under the train
but apparently that's what bones sound like when
torn rattling out of flesh, fortunately
the open window doesn't promise any new havoc
democracy promises everyone a holy card
and for some of us a bust as well

———

put what you wanted to wave back in a motionless hand
on your toes you can still see an opposite shore behind you, just there
in the distance a bird still and the rocky promontory nobody
ran out onto to stand on the end on their toes waving
waving until their hand has wiped you out of the view
don't turn back again, soon you will forget the bird and the gestures
forgetting there wasn't anybody on the rocky promontory, eyes never
win out long over distance, but just now in the distance you still saw –

Thirst

Running, always running, foolishly away from the herd
running full tilt into a garish wish for distance, smashing yourself
to smithereens on mountains on the ice caps
on a lover's eyes, nothing ceded

nobody irons the shirts anymore or the man underneath them
and creases turn into rips so fast, rips rapidly turning into a raw wound
until it falls from the wardrobe

the object engaged with becoming an object constantly pushes
its borders with no prospect of that pushing ever
changing it into a larger form

are origins and where we are rushing
paratactic to our attempts to take up space
yelling our presence on a back seat with our nails in the leather
of shoulders or a car seat

suffering creature or object or trussed beast, you are lighter
than your cumbersome form suggests

and you know people generally do not meet
an insect snaps so easily
between the boredom of two fingers

and we just break
out of each other's ribs, letting our will-less limbs dangle
as if a much larger adversary has us by the scruff of the neck

distance turns out to be the TV test card, you are locked
in the taste of how he remembers your mouth
not chafed or cracked, without promises or lipstick, blood oranges

you remember before the murmuring the block letters proclaim you
but which voice still knows your name, so loud
so urgent and how long will it last, the flickering
of what is already faltering
and hardly makes the surface

the way that breath on exertion sometimes keeps panting under the skin
not making it through the mouth, swelling inside to an airless bulge
that makes you think nothing can escape

as long as your skin doesn't turn blue to refute the opposite
you are not transparent, you smother
what used to dry in yellow rings in the lampshade at home

you sit there
shattering yourself from the inside out

you count the ribs, now without pollen
nobody breaks out of you

the butchered remains pile up like an elephants' graveyard in the living-room
where you wait between the bones and the prams
for a dead man you already know by rote

constant thirst, a chamois in your mouth, self-preservation
starts with wrists around wrists truncated
you wring your way into someone else, a weir

until men in orange overalls dig up the water pipes
gigantic umbilical cords
in search of the stone
you know is in your stomach

since your mother thirteen and sliding down the downpipe
slipping away from the pub on the square with the dice tray
and the goat drunk on a rope, slipping away

from the guy at the bar, his whole life
just back from Thailand, he says you have beautiful slanty eyes
mosquito bites on your breast already

the mirror shows the far side of yourself, somewhat shy nipples
block letters on your knickers saying m o n d a y

how disconsolate still: every attempt that becomes a series
despite all resolutions an animal species
that has given up on reproduction
not necessarily lonely, but delivered up
to an instinct that has forgotten its compulsion

this is what you learnt:
at battles only mourn the slaughtered horses
'enough tears have been shed for the people already'

also: you have a soul
that has exactly the same shape as your body
of slightly smaller girth, so it can slide under your skin
holding the organs together in an amniotic sac
when you have to howl

also: what older men have in common
is that they all get a racing bike
your father too, for whom you once made a clay
statue of Osama bin Laden, he thought
it was beautiful and wasn't the least bit offended

kept it on the side table, only later do you learn
what an idol can do to a living-room
a man wants to cycle away from on Sundays

and that doesn't matter
absence is a kind of bond

so you ran, constantly
and naked with your thirst and your rejection
you would never reach the mountain
nor the sharp ice caps, the blue panting
already pushing under your skin, constantly you walk

without having moved, you sit there
rubbed dry with a towel
and wedged among your own kind

between the open lips your name is no longer on
that have stopped being a mouth
and become a wound

Section

Monday, Yellow (Pastel)

July, pale heat, fingers dripping from my wrists, finding
shadow in eyes behind sunglasses aimed at me
in late and changing afternoon light
I expect at least three shades from the water

it is too constrained here
in the liquid dot my hesitant body becomes by accident
in other people's photos

the map stretches a paper skin over Paris
along the folds the streets bulge up
like bent backbones poking through T-shirts

I keep my steps and my balance
the way you used to use your knuckles
to work out the long and short months, a grip

has been gettable since the idea of time encloses a wrist
so why do I stagger

behind the blue water lies a dark bed
behind the blue sky a dark universe
the world has a false bottom that will break the fall

wasteful in the end
like the provisional lovers dining here alfresco

Tuesday, Green, Rust

under me a line on a map rolls into a street name
on a route that will soon become the distance I covered to the cross, where
the covered distance changes to a crossed-off area

I can demarcate as a place that fits
into the four corners of my vision, looking
at a city through a View-Master is safe, transparency
after transparency after transparency clicks the impressions into
your eyes your mind, not together at least

but I'm getting ahead of myself, for now
I'm blindly searching for barbs that will catch
a later homebound step, I'm not even on my way
and already thinking myself back

my forward-moving feet and resistant
thoughts lean me back until I'm flat
on the esplanade waiting for a direction

no matter how long I lie there, no one
chalks a line around me, all too slowly
the cramp turns back into my body

Wednesday, Peach

standing on the corner of the street is the left half of a woman
she doesn't know where she's got to
but that's okay, she says
you can pull yourself together in cross-section

this place is crawling
with cosmopolitans and castaways
I am one and then the other, half each
maybe never more than an impulse of myself

fickle things follow a definite course, they pass

still the meltwater from a day in Paris sets again
in the morning's monochrome beauty

quietly the white stones stack up as buildings
that don't yet need to fit

the eye's expectation and briefly
I can think unobserved

ah, is there a girl left who still just dreams of a boy on a motorbike
sure, for a moment
and never

Thursday, Greyish Blue

today you overwhelmed me in three faces on the streets
it was like starting to think of breathing, irreversible
and something you only thought about just in time

now you are afraid
to stop thinking about the movement of your lungs
because you think your lungs will stop then too

because the postcard slides over the view so quickly
like the view over distance and at night the distant darkness
over people, I don't even

know how fast skin and polyester bind
to personal enamel, how much crust

before someone becomes a part of a building
a sliding background for passers-by, or why

my grandmother used the names of previous dogs to call her Jack Russell
so often she forgot his

so I don't call out to your faces
and stop giving names to strangers

Friday, Electric Blue

it kept going, the flickering of the people
between the lights, the constant throb
of the city inside me, the taste of aniseed
diluted with evening and remorse, scant in the corner of a mouth

I choke
on some old French, in the mixed colours of many and the same faces
honey in the whisky, yesterday

a meteorite exploded over Europe in low tones
the sound travelled around the Earth three times
but we didn't hear it

deaf and dumb the stars dangle in the sky and the words
between two mouths that won't break open
are interchangeable

Saturday, Magenta

past the hip-swinging scents in Goutte d'Or
with the languid tread of a lithe tiger

late in the afternoon letting my eyes
slide lazily to the sides of my head

further along a hand crumbles into clattering kola nuts
in a bowl of bare fingers, maize, maize, maize
a man on repeat aims me

as mechanically as a chomping mouth
I walk up the stairs of the Sacré-Coeur
like Pac-Man through a maze

hunger is the tepid kiss of a stranger
who says that being tired's okay
now the city's curling up grey and contained in a corner

and I, eroded by one-off glances
am still searching for the view
that will raise looking over wanting

at the top the church turns out to be an umbrella and salvation
a plastic poncho

Sunday, Ochre

it was too little and dead tired before it began, shy mouth
with just twenty-six stubborn letters, leftover
lemon tart and cigarettes, the sameness

hidden in possible versions
a city can assume from its map

morning and again that same maquette, empty poems
and streets I don't need to invent a way back for

I wanted this
skeleton of external lines, a stylised light in the afternoon

and in the middle the neckline of a dress
and that should say it all

but eyes too are flexible
and everything got tangled
rushing together

without the precision of a scar
leaving a story

Fricative

A step to the left
and you fall off the page, lie there
out of sight, out of shot of screams and deceit

lie there with all that's pale and asleep and will
not be written and stay

there, quiet and pretending
and reinforced along the seam
that runs between story and aorta

you still have to be so many people for me
you still have to

Hypostasis

Out of the white a swipe, a letter
struck against the dragging pointlessness

almost what we'd wanted to say, somewhere
between the cerebral cortex and intent and outcome
the mouth becomes a gag

and thoughts can be so sharp, the mind
a cutlery drawer, I'm not among the spoons
but on the blade side of what drives thinking to a point, the poem
more blur than word, candlewax solidified as fever
every collapsed lung its colour and adjective

swallow the voice too
it always starts with the refusal
to give length and breadth to a moment

but continues all the same
so curl the body up like a comma
after an exclamation or a supplication, it doesn't matter which
there will be a place, a gasp long

Slash and Burn

Take me with you,

I have learnt the names of the trees now
the birch, the maple, the redwood: a shadow
that thought us possible, how little
can eyelids really cover, the autumn
still long

and even with eyes closed I will see it before me
how the rain fell through us, becoming
injury

melancholy and its load capacity, tired tissue
that's overstretched

I am unattached

Take me with you,

I know the names of the trees now and better
than to want to swap truth
for certainty, how little

does a shadow differ from a closed eye
from a scorch mark, the image of us

burnt to a fibre, but for a long time
into all that will come I'll see it before me

the man with your face, he's grinding a dull wish to make a knife
the man with your face, he strikes matches on my knees
and tells me I am the pilot light

of his grief, blow it out
leave blaze and mask uncharged

Take me with you,

the house is longing for prayer and presence, there are months
dripping in the dishrack, shards scrubbed and rinsed and you don't come
floor mopped with bleach and you don't set a foot

what needed cleaning
gleams too late, the few conceded days have passed

I add intention to mistake
make an incubator of ribs and reeds, and somewhere
in a jaw I wait

until the diminutives are ripe, until
the resident coughs up cement and stops
being a wall

Take me with you,

now the house is craving return
a craving that has long since withered in us
whimpering walls and what of it? nowhere

were we rubbed so hard into the floor, nowhere
our names on the bell, a first letter
a year, nowhere

preserving what in time
and through failure was meant
to become life, a mausoleum
of patchouli and vanilla candles

but a smell can't raise a room
whimpering walls, come back
lay your hand on the deficiencies, come

and tell the walls that they
were only bruises

Take me with you,

the ground is exhausted, the body
did its best as a lover and a sickbed
time and again with fever dancing in your veins
the body laid you down to sleep in soft corners

you dreamt of a bright shining angel
you carried it up a mountain
when it had given up, when the sun smashed
to pieces on the white cliffs and blinded

the body gave you shade
a hiding place, you were so keen
to disappear into it, entirely

until you recovered and your recovery the place
you knew: this is where the body must be discarded

White

Rolled up in the afternoon in the duvet in my hocked body
sinking into the soft centimetre
before I fold double, soon

the first fish will crawl out of the water again, I will bear
the light again, warm in the afternoon again
in your peach skin

and the fruit is juicy, I can already hear the wasps in the distance
Mendeleev is ordering the elements
we will know everything, painting the room white over and over
to stop the flesh of the walls from showing

the burst capillaries
throb behind the picture frames, soon

the bang in the desert will come, the hair on your chest
in a mushroom cloud and it doesn't matter
what I now become
a life with a front garden, a Play-Doh Venus

the eye has already spilt a stain on the ceiling
hardly green at all but I know it's green
– I know the stain from before

a dark centre appears in the patch of colour
giving it a gaping mouth, approaching
what is awake is being swallowed

someone cuts five fingers into my hand
I am no longer an observer
the tattered thoughts of us that afternoon in a skin
and the soft centimetre, nothing

stays still long enough to merge into itself
we're better off falling apart
into possible versions of the same thing

like the continents
putting oceans between them

deep in the stain in the nightmare in the mouth
a pale mountaintop is breathing beneath us
breathing in the duvet the centuries that have worn
the mountain out of the landscape

and no matter how heavy, how red the sky as well
for a moment it no longer feels
like my limbs will break off

everything is thin and alone
and fingers are just frayed skin
your threadbare extremities

that's why people make fists
a blind hem to contain themselves
didn't you know that?

doubt, a reckless word
but there is the consolation
that things will pale of their own accord, later

what I can't forget will be part
of the little superfluities of a collected life

as keen as I was to pick shells out of the sand's backbone
back home they're only the bones of a fleeting interest

let the fruit and the afternoon and your ripe mouth
go the same way: random objects
in memory's flea market, nothing

in the dark in the turning in the biting green
of the stain lessens, the nightmare gapes

like your final face back then, the pale moment
in which your mouth could no longer
hold the words

on top of the belly of the mountain in the red moss
I puff up and burst in the breathing soil
a breath growing more frantic and mine
and I think: I'm falling

but there is no whole no depth no edge

I fall into myself through myself
through your skin, the gravel, the graze
through the peremptory voice that says
I must become myself, later

the air has pushed me heavy and red
into the moss into the duvet into the stone
and the mountain swallows me

before morning comes I turn into a crevice, a crack
in the merciless bedrock

I am a place that doesn't exist
a place light pushes through

Topos

Where we found it? under a willow by a stream
in the nettles between the daisies and purple orchids
as if death is that serene

sliding down the bank, light grey leaves, flakes of skin
a tangle of hair and algae, a deserter floating
on the surface, over the course of days

waterlogging weight dragged it down into the mud
a final bed in a shallow below, until it couldn't float
away again, until suddenly it was lying in our hands

lying in our hands with such brazen vulnerability
who can we blame for that?

There

Standing backlit on the roof is a man
sniper of my thoughts, he hears it all

the rages and the silences
the secret heavy breathing
from my teenage bedroom, the escape plans

sometimes he's a neighbour, sometimes an enemy or a saviour
more often just a blur that's blocking the sun

and I know it takes no courage
to stand on the roof, one step out
to the ground that makes so much teeter

but he is a lens and in charge
the naked eye observing
our incapacity to belong together

It's not that I haven't thought about it: ways of escaping
the closed shutter, the carotid artery, reluctant love
away from a father or an omniscient narrator
– maybe that's the same thing: both concealed in the story

I wasn't afraid of the fist through the wall, it made a breathing hole
in the house, the fear came later
with the painting they hung over the hole, a blue hydrangea
in a round vase of casual brushstrokes, as if the fist had never been there

les fleurs nous protègent, les fleurs et les bougies, says a little boy on the news
the memory of least resistance; despite the scab on the language
hunched one after the other around the kitchen table, shoulders up
to take silence's battering, despite the dear waxen mother
transformed into a candle just for us

resolved to become the hole in the wall, loud, incorrigible
throbbing behind the painting, both breath and aberration

becoming the painting after all, a shape for the wound

Mother looks at the hollyhocks
and thinks of the pea in her throat
that has nowhere to go except deeper
into her lungs

is it still there
or has it dissolved by itself in the meantime, how long
will the hollyhocks keep thinking themselves up?

Mother watches a tired bud
leave the plant between the blades of the secateurs
falling into the grass, so abandoned
you could confuse death with lying down

Mother snaps two roses with brown edges
it's my brother and me that time
he led me blindfold across the lawn, deliberately
aiming for the wall

Mother waters the hollyhocks, mentally
sopping my knees in iodine
years later she'll try to trim the scars from the garden

Grandfather collected the coupons from the Quick
saving up our six-monthly get-together
at a motorway restaurant

each time his nose looked more like a potato
the purple veins and craters: bulwark
of the years

spent drinking his skin to leather
he bought me an aquarium for my First Communion
and a land tortoise

now I'm a vegetarian, all we have left
is a woozy blood tie, a sea shanty
he once taught me:

Oh, the captain of the good ship Finnegar, drowned hisself in a bottle of vinegar

even the tortoise found it too miserable in this house
preferring the compost heap at the bottom of the garden
to hibernate

After school in the brown leatherette lounge room
Grandmother turned the heating up to unbearable
she wore a pink dressing gown over the clothes
under which daughters divided into daughters

I sat at the kitchen table as one of her fractions
knowing young that we were women who were a remainder from nothing
and remaining from nothing is enough

you can always tell poor people, she said
from the way they spread raw mince
on their sandwiches

she made me fry the meat to resist identification
because things don't just happen to us, she said
people do what happens to them too

later I'll explain the difference between breasts and bread, she said
otherwise all you need to know is what to say
when things go wrong or the weather's bad

rain, rain, go away
come again some other day

They say there's only one direction you can take from here, away
and once you've gone you soon find out that the world there is no bigger
than the world the newspapers here speak scandal of
a bad habit of ours the catechism tried to break

but if you grow up at the end of the line no one needs to tell you
that where things end there is always a consequence
reversed, like the palm of a hand
as if we were asking for it, how often

do you have to go away before you can turn back and how often
do you come back until you can call it staying?

what is there to leave behind anyway, a first love
overshadowed steeples, the chain of our surnames
– as if we could ever lose them, those twisted vowels

the space cakes we made for each other's birthdays
to lay claim to a night in our hometown
where autumn after summer after spring we only became metonyms
for the selves we were insisting on in other places

You'd Like to Build a Boat

You would like to build a boat

you draw up a plan of the kind of boat
you would like to build
the plan goes into a plastic sleeve in a folder
so that later in the workshop it doesn't get dirty

you make a back-up plan
in case you do something like pour a cup of coffee over it
this plan is important
it puts you in control during the boatbuilding

first you build the boat from cardboard:
you draw rectangles on the cardboard to represent standard sheets of plywood
inside the rectangles you draw to scale the sections of the boat's outside structure
you cut the sections out of the cardboard and tape them together

do they not fit?
try until they fit

do they not fit?
be glad you've made a mistake
later you won't make the mistake again with the real material

keep trying until they fit

then you can commence your search
for plywood with the right dimensions, thickness and price – don't buy rubbish!
at the same time buy the required amount of fibreglass and epoxy resin

now you can start building

you put the drawing of the plan on the plywood
you measure it all out
you check the measurements twice – maybe calling in a second pair of eyes
it's easy to make a mistake

you construct a building frame to attach the frames
at exactly the right separation
always using a spirit level

screw/nail the plywood panels onto the frames
you drill pairs of holes in abutting panels
and sew them together with copper wire, loosely at first
is the boat still level? only then do you pull the stitches tight

you fill the seams with epoxy and reinforce them with fibreglass
now you can remove the stitches, feel how solid it is
the wood would break before the seam
the joint is strong and durable

now the inside too
you attach the frames to the hull
after that you have to do the wiring, put in benches, build the cabin
attach the rubbing strakes, mount the motor plate, raise a mast

only then can the nails and screws be definitively removed
make sure to fill all the holes of course
a layer of fibreglass on the outside
makes the boat even stronger, even more durable

give all the wood another coat of epoxy
the boat is now watertight, finally apply filler and sand the boat
choose a good paint for the finish

the boat is now ready
where to go?